To Richa[...] W9-BMU-062
With Love
on our Spiritual
Journey together...

Love,
Koula

Tao

sacred symbols

Tao

Thames and Hudson

THE LAND OF
THREE RELIGIONS

In pre-Communist China three great religions flourished, or perhaps it would be more true to term them as two religions and one way of life. The first was Confucianism, an austere and élitist body of belief of especial appeal to the Mandarin classes. Buddhism was the second, practised in many varieties by a multitude of sects. In some instances it had become little more than a system of popular magic; in this aspect it tended to overlap with some of the simpler forms of Taoism, the third great system of belief and experience. Unlike the others, this was not a set system with a central god, but a way of guidance for man.

Frontispiece A silk canopy with dragons, symbols of celestial *yang* essences, China, 16th/17th century.

Right Lao-tzu and Confucius take care of the future Buddha, Sākyamuni, silk painting, China, 14th century.

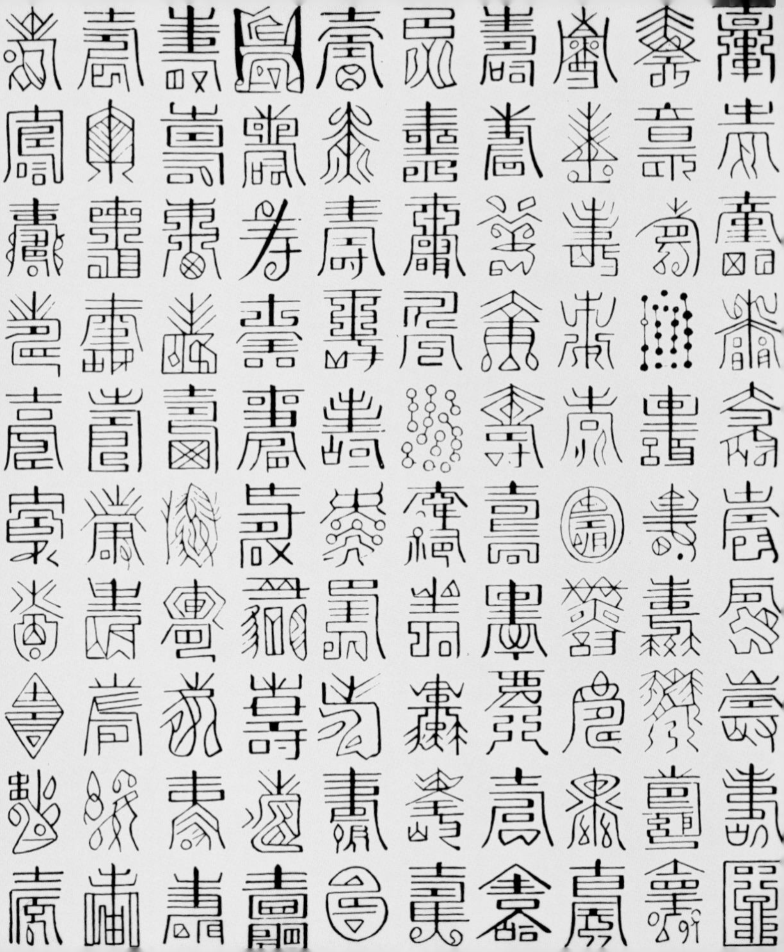

ONE PICTURE IS WORTH
A THOUSAND WORDS

taoism is rooted in symbolism; the very characters of the Chinese languages are themselves potent symbols, which may also reflect the individual spirit of the writer. Calligraphy itself – the movement of the brush across the paper – symbolizes the flow of vital currents through the universe, the threads of linear continuity which the Taoist perceives as the energizing elements of the cosmos. Secret scripts of great beauty have been developed by Taoists to express the working forces of heaven and earth both by reference and meaning and also by the form of the characters.

Above The character *shou* ('long life') resembles the diagram for the 'three crucibles' internal circulation of the Taoist adept, rubbing, China, 19th century.
Opposite One hundred talismanic forms of the character *shou*.

TAO

'Tao' defies translation and
complete definition. According
to one ancient inscription, it is
'the ancestor of all doctrines,
the mystery beyond mysteries'.
Sometimes inadequately rendered
in English as 'the Way', the Tao
informs all phenomena, but can
only be seen through symbol –
the flowing of water, the sexual
act, the awakening of the psychic
centres of the body, valley and
mountains, where the ideal
Taoist may dwell in communion
with the heavens.

The Taoist adept holds open a scroll prominently
embellished with the *yin/yang* symbol, silk panel,
China, Ming Dynasty, 14th/17th century.

the three profound studies

The story of the development of Taoism is a strange one; its deepest principles are those of openness and accommodation, reflected in the non-doctrinal nature of the basic texts, the three great works: the Tao te ching, the Chuang-tzu and the I-ching.

Through allusion and suggestion, the first introduces the Tao, the way to harmony. The Chuang-tzu goes further in resolving the position of man in relation to the natural world. The I-ching (Book of Changes) is a practical oracle book, a list of possibilities, but never a work of definite instruction.

The great works of Taoism advise the seeker after knowledge and harmony to identify the vital energies of the universe, represented as a three-dimensional landscape on this bronze jar (China, Western Han Dynasty, 209–206 B.C.) (*opposite*) and as never-ending flow on a celadon dish (*left*), China, Ming Dynasty, 14th century.

'The Tao which can be described cannot be the true Tao, which is nameless.' – *Lao-tzu*

lao-tzu and the tao te ching

the basic document of Taoist thought, the Tao te ching, is one of remarkable shortness; compared with the lengthy texts of most of the world's systems of belief, it is a work of great compression. The short fragments of which it is composed are pieces of great subtlety and complexity, relying more on suggestion than description and asking more questions than providing answers. Sometimes known as 'the book of five thousand characters', it is generally attributed to Lao-tzu, a Chinese sage and a contemporary of Confucius, and acquired book form c. 4th century B.C.

The great Taoist sage: a tenth-century rock carving of Lao-tzu, Fujian, China (*opposite*). He was also often shown on a water buffalo, symbolizing his flight from corruption (*below*), bronze statuette, China, Ming Dynasty, 17th century.

無上玄元三天玉堂大法

諸將符

天地人神
立派之精

行遍天下
敕殺鬼神

二十八宿

助明運符

上天下地無所不經歷
應機押入凡心神君

the two lines

because of its lack of an organizational
structure Taoism did not develop a church
in the sense that other great religions have
done, and consequently it has tended to
manifest itself in varied forms. One of these,
known as the Way of the Heavenly Teacher,
was probably little more than a folk religion.
But there was also another way, of greater self-discipline,
of physical and mental exercise, of refinement of the
body and spirit, of devotion to a proper
understanding of ebb and flow. For the
true adept of the second line, the ideal
examples were the Immortals, the hsien.

Tao sages study a scroll with the *yin/yang* symbol
(*opposite left*), China, Ch'ing Dynasty (1644–1912), the most subtle
form of Taoism; the Heavenly Messenger, represented here
talismanically, was believed in popular Taoism to walk the
earth killing evil spirits (*opposite right*).

the hsien

the Immortals of Taoism were, in many ways, ordinary beings writ large. Their power was derived not so much from innate divinity as from observing the correct way in all things and thus arriving at superhuman understanding and – often – immortality. Although some were believed to ride through the air on cranes and dragons to join the heavenly imperial court, the majority about whom the ancient stories were told lived on earth on such symbolically charged substances as cinnabar and fungus, thereby partaking of the universal energies of yang and yin.

Winged dragons and *hsien*, denoting closeness to the heavens (*above*), bas-relief, China, Han Dynasty, 3rd century B.C./A.D. 3rd century. 'Red Robe' (*opposite*), a papier-mâché figure, one of six to twelve which line the Path to Heaven in the Taoist ritual of Presenting the Memorial to the Jade Emperor, southern Taiwan.

shou-lao

many of the
hsien *are associated with
the most potent symbolism of the
Tao. Almost every association carries rich
significance in the delicate balancing of inner and
outer forces and influences. Shou-lao, god of longevity,
was the personification of maleness and of the* yang *essences.
He was therefore often associated with the dragon and the
crane, symbols of longevity attained by well-controlled
sexual and meditational lives. Some representations
show the Immortal holding a peach, a* yin *symbol
whose cleft was seen to be evocative of the
female vulva and the delights which
this could afford men.*

Longevity is associated in the *Tao te
ching* with suppleness and non-action, pliancy
and fragility, in contrast to hardness and
boldness which result in death.

The bald-headed god of longevity, Shou-lao, one of the most eminent of male *hsien*, holds up a scripture scroll and a peach, symbol of the long life, painting on paper, China, Ch'ing Dynasty, 17th/20th century.

Legendary queen of the West, symbolic figure of *yin* energies, the *hsien* Hsi-wang-mu is represented in this sixteenth-century Chinese silk painting with a phoenix, potent symbol of *yang* energies.

hsi-wang-mu

althought the figure
of Shou-lao shows his
closeness to yin energies in
his bearing of the peach, it seems
appropriate that his undoubted
yang potency should be counterbalanced
by Hsi-wang-mu, the Queen of the Peach-
garden Paradise in the West. Although
this female Immortal may very well be
shown carrying an offering dish,
symbol of female sexuality and
therefore of yin energies, ultimate harmony
may be conveyed by the presence of a powerful
yang symbol, such as the phoenix.

Lao-tzu refers to the entrance of the
female as 'the root of heaven and earth'.

secret harmonies

Whether expressed in the tales of the Immortals, of saintly lives lived in mountain sanctuaries or among a celestial bestiary, or whether through the thoughtful conduct of the everyday, the aim of Taoism in life and art is harmony. The emblems and iconography of traditional Chinese art are symbols of a balancing of forces, of the yang and the yin, observation of which will itself induce feelings of contentment. In the widest sense there is the balance to be sought between the fundamental ebb and flow of the universe, the male and female principles, the forms of permanence and the forms of change.

The unity of all things – Heaven, Earth and Man – is symbolized in this bowl (*yin*) decorated with penis forms (*yang*), China, Ming Dynasty, 16th century. Similar unity is expressed in the trigrams of the *pi* disc (*above*): Heaven, wave and rocks are crossed by the shaft symbolizing Earth, China, Ming Dynasty, 15th/16th century.

YIN YANG

t he principle of polarity is at the heart
of Taoist thought. Yet this emphasis
on opposites must not be mistaken for
a situation of conflict – everything implies
its opposite and, indeed, is only
meaningful because the opposite is
there. And so, death and life, light
and darkness, good and evil,
positive and negative, ebb and
flow, male and female coexist
as parts of one and the same system.
The elimination of either one
would also mean the
disappearance of the other.

'Something and Nothing produce
each other.' – *Lao-tzu*.

A painted panel with the *yin/yang* symbol surrounded by trigrams
made up of *yin* (broken) and *yang* (whole) lines.

血湖地獄燈圖　　九宮八卦士燈圖　　　火德燈圖　　九天玉樞燈圖

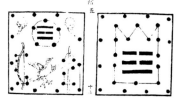

i-ching

Of all the three great texts the I-ching – the Book of Changes – comes closest to being a manual for the Taoist. Its origins are shrouded in mystery and, although thought to be of great antiquity, it is mentioned by neither Lao-tzu nor Chuang-tzu and probably originated as a body of orally transmitted folk wisdom. It differs from all other oracular texts in regarding the past, present and future as a dynamic entity, flowing and changing and therefore not susceptible to strict instruction or law-making. The permutations of the yin/yang forces are worked out in terms of 64 line hexagrams, each composed of two trigrams made up of broken (yin) and unbroken (yang) lines.

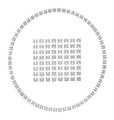

The gate of the Heaven which comes after the beginning of time, in a contemporary Taoist temple (*opposite above*); the trigrams which surround it represent new energy entering the world. The continued interaction of *yin* and *yang* (*opposite below* and *above*) in trigrammatic form.

consulting the oracle

The consultation of magic diagrams to obtain guidance is a practice central to Taoism; here, the Emperor prepares to divine the future by means of yarrow stalks (*opposite*); other diagrams may be made up of randomly assorted objects or formally arranged trigrams (*above*).

the I-ching may be consulted in three ways; the most venerated is the fifty sticks technique, but six wands or six coins may be used. The book itself should be placed on a table free from other objects and laid on a clean piece of cloth. In Taoism it is believed that the source of wisdom lies in the north and the table should therefore be positioned in the northernmost part of the room and approached from the south. An incense barrier may be placed by the sticks, wands or coins. The question to be asked should be seriously held in mind; the random sorting of the objects will give the enquirer the lines of two trigrams, leading to the relevant text.

colour and design

the *polarities of* yin *and* yang *are the articulating principles of traditional Chinese art. Constant interaction of the two provides the meaning of countless paintings, wall-hangings and designs on clothing and even on domestic pottery. The juxtaposition of certain colours expresses the balance of essential forces (*yang *colours first): red/blue, red/green, white/black, gold/silver. Certain types of artefact, perhaps more closely associated with a single sex, may express one force more strongly; porcelain and soapstone are more strongly identified with the female side of the household and are therefore decorated with* yin *symbols, such as baskets and fungus.*

An unusual silk panel (*opposite*) woven in contrasting colours with a phoenix and crane design, China, Ming Dynasty, 15th century. Although a *yang* symbol, the phoenix was also an emblem of the Empress.

cosmos

taoism is underwritten by the sense of the cyclical, by a worldview which sees everything in relation to everything else. There can be no 'before' unless there is an 'after'; in the words of Lao-tzu: 'From Tao arises one; from one arises two; from two arises three; and from three arise the ten thousand things.' The symbolic representations of the world therefore balance the yin/yang forces: the east may be symbolized by a green dragon (yang *rising*), the south by a phoenix (yang *at its height*), the west by a white tiger (yin *rising*), and north by a tortoise entwined with a serpent (yin *dominant*).

This nineteenth-century Japanese bronze of entwined tortoise and serpent (*yin*), which also have the attributes of dragon and tiger (*yang*), and the animal figures of this seventeenth-century Chinese mirror (*opposite*) symbolize the unity of the Taoist cosmos.

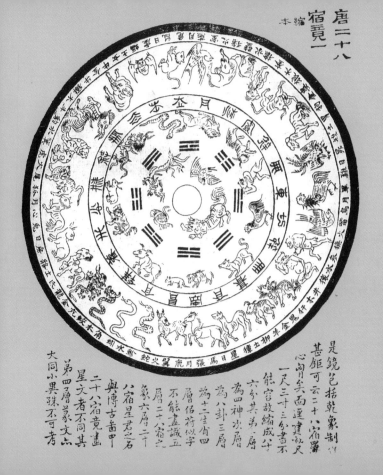

是鏡包括乾象制作
甚鉅可云面運二十八宿羅
心闊尖西運建於口
一尺三十三分晝不
能容故縮成半
六分共其第二層
為四神次層
為十二生肖四
層為八卦三層
層似符似字
不能盡識五
層二十八宿之
象六角二十
八宿星君之名
與博古畫中
二十八宿竟畫
星文者不同其
第四層蒙文點
大同小異殊不可考

Cosmic energy is symbolized by the pearl, pursued by a blue (*yin*) dragon against a red (*yang*) background, silk panel, Chinese, 16th/17th century.

'Heaven: the high it sets lower; the low it raises.' – *Lao-tzu*.

the jade heavens

heaven and earth are themselves symbols of the yin/yang polarity. Inertness and receptivity are perceived as earthly, yin characteristics, while the heavens are the concentration of vital, yang energies. The symbolism even extended to traditional Chinese coinage — the circle (heaven) pierced by the square (earth); the circle symbolism for heaven was repeated in the pi disc which, like many other amulets, was often made of jade. Other stones were regarded as essence of earth, but jade, the semen of celestial dragons, was essence of heaven.

A *pi* disc (*opposite*), made of jade, was decorated with embossed points to symbolize the constellations, China, *c.* 3rd century B.C.

Movements of the heavens were of constant fascination to the early Taoist; in this Han Dynasty relief (*below*) an officer of the court of Ursa Major sits in a chariot, symbolizing the constellation, accompanied by phoenix and dragon.

the five earthly elements

五行旗　金木水火土五面各照五行之色

although the
mutual interdependence
of the elements of the universe is
expressed as yin and yang, early Taoism
also expressed the cyclical nature of the world in terms
of the Five Elements. According to the teaching of Tsou-
yen (c. 350–270 B.C.), a scholar from the north-
east of China, wood gives rise to fire, from
which ash gives rise to earth, from whose depths
is mined metal, whose polished surface may
attract dew (water), which causes wood to
grow and thus to complete the cycle.

A peach-shaped box (*opposite*) decorated with a variety of
lucky emblems to signify the harmony of the elements of the
universe, China, Ch'ing Dynasty, 18th century.

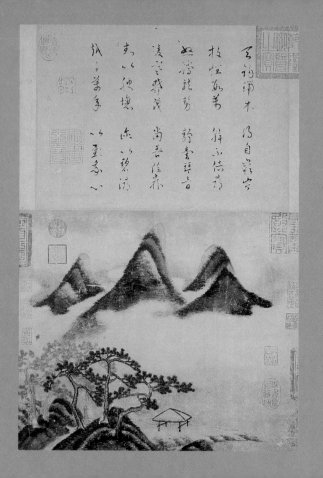

the landscape of harmony

the Tao is the essential course of nature; it is the way things are, the universal principle of order. It is expressed in the combination of natural phenomena — the relationship of mountains and valleys, of land and water, height and depth, convex and concave forms. In landscape painting, the Taoist artist will try to convey the harmonies in his subject by picking out the subtle connections between the shapes of earth formations. Mountains may be shown marked by 'dragon veins' — currents of yang energy running through the otherwise inert yin of the earth.

符形真嶽北

嶽北

The importance of mountains: a talismanic symbol of the five great mountain peaks (*above*), the source of the five elements; *Spring Mountains and Pine Trees* is a supremely harmonious painting by Mi Fei (1051–1107).

A wooden stand carved with waves (*opposite*), China, Ch'ing Dynasty, 1769; *In Front of the Waterfall* (*left*) by Ma Lin shows sages contemplating a waterfall, while the climbing tree symbolizes the tenacity of the scholars, ink on silk, *c.* 1246.

Water is identified in the *Tao te ching* as being the element closest to the highest good: it does not contend with the many creatures and plants which it nourishes; it flows into places where no being would wish to be. In these qualities it comes close to being a complete symbol of the Tao. It is submissive and weak, yet it can successfully attack what is strong and hard.

the good of water

although the Tao is the order of the universe,
it is a very different order from the rigid
concepts of Western culture. This organic
order is most perfectly symbolized by
water, the weakest element yet the strongest:
'It is thus that Tao in the world is like a
river going down the valley to the ocean' (Lao-tzu).
It takes the form of clouds and mist,
the very breath of the yin earth,
and returns as rain, bringing yang
energy to fill the river and
oceans, finding
the lines of flow in the
landscape. The way it moves is
a potent symbol of the vital patterns
of the universe; the way it stands
still expresses peace and understanding.

the veins in the stone

the swirling, unpredictable flow of energy so clearly seen in water is noted by the Taoist adept in many other forms — smoke and incense rising, for instance. Such forceful veins are also reproduced in much Chinese ceramic and metal ware in the form of marbling or streaking, or in the arrangement of coloured blotches. The true Taoist will find greatest satisfaction in the streaking or veining of rocks and stones, perhaps themselves worn and pitted by the steady erosion of water. Stones shaped by water have the true quality of the Tao; their irregularity suggests the interpenetration of yang and yin and, as such, are eagerly collected by the adept.

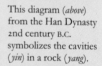

青城山 一名 天國山

This diagram (*above*) from the Han Dynasty 2nd century B.C. symbolizes the cavities (*yin*) in a rock (*yang*).

The forms of wood, too, provide the Taoist with a potent source of solid/cavity symbolism (*opposite*), woodcut illustrating the 9th-century love story of Ts'ui Ying-ying.

歘火會雷霆大作雷電大作折樹誅妖孽雨傾盆

cinnabar

In the Taoist symbolism of substances, jade and cinnabar stand out. Jade, we have seen, is closely associated with the celestial dragon and, therefore, with yang *forces. But cinnabar is an even more potent symbol, expressing nothing less than the joining of* yin *and* yang. *Composed largely of sulphide of mercury it provides red pigment for painting, but in Taoist magic it was regarded – sometimes too literally – as the elixir of life. In the Inner Alchemy of Taoism it came to represent the achieving of the ultimate spiritual state, the awakening of all the subtle energies of the body to bring the devotee into the most perfect harmony with the universe.*

A valued and highly symbolic pigment, cinnabar is here combined with ink to illustrate the combination of fire and cloud in a Taoist almanac, China, 19th century (*opposite*).

peach, peony and chrysanthemum

the softer, more yielding character of plant life and its obviously close dependence on the earth gives it especially strong yin associations. Examples would be used in Chinese art to symbolize the female element in the balance of harmonies in the whole composition. Flower decoration, for instance, might be used on tableware so that yin qualities would be absorbed by the food served on it. A garden of peony flowers, the setting for an intimate domestic scene, might be counterbalanced by the swooping form of a Fen-bird (yang). The Immortal Hsi-wang-mu lives in the Peach Garden (a female sexual symbol) but may be accompanied by the distinctly male phoenix.

Plant and fruit symbolism in Taoist art is complex and varied; much of it refers to sexual vitality, as in both these illustrations: peaches painted on a porcelain bowl (*opposite*), China, 18th century; stone rubbing of plum blossom in winter (*right*), China, 14th century.

Porcelain vase (*opposite*), a
yin symbol, decorated with
spirit fungus, symbol of a
long life and of the benefits
of sexual intercourse, China,
20th century; cloud fungus
is associated with an
Immortal (*left*) in this
hardstone carving, China,
Ming Dynasty, 17th century.

fungus

the seemingly unpredictable, soft character of fungus makes it a powerful expression of the yin essence. So important is it in the Taoist world-view that the traditional hat – 'the fragrant cap' – worn by the true adept takes its main form from fungoid growth; it will then be decorated with objects of yang significance. One image of the goddess Lan Tsai-ho, surrounded by clouds (yin), shows her accompanied by a stag (yang) whose maleness is mitigated by his bearing yin fungus in his mouth. Those mushrooms which share the concave, swirling forms of fungi also symbolize yin essences. But cone-shaped mushrooms – suggesting the phallus – are regarded as potently yang.

dragon and phoenix

there is a satisfying serenity in the yin/yang
polarity, the effect of balance throughout all
observable worlds, both natural and
mythical. Yang is symbolized by
beasts which appear aggressive and male,
notably the stallion, the ram, the cock and,
most especially, the dragon, emblem of the Emperor.
It is also a powerful sexual symbol of
penetration, appearing in representations of
the 'Leaping White Tiger' position, or
'Attack from the Rear'. Other symbolic
beasts are the reindeer, rhinoceros, the Feng-bird
and phoenix. The latter is a common
counterpoint in garden scenes to the yin
properties of the peach, the open basket or the bowl.

Dragon and tiger (*opposite left*), symbols of heaven and
earth, woodcut, Japan, 18th century; dragon-fish glazed ceramic
finial (*opposite right*) from the roof of a Taoist temple,
China, Ch'ing Dynasty, 19th century.

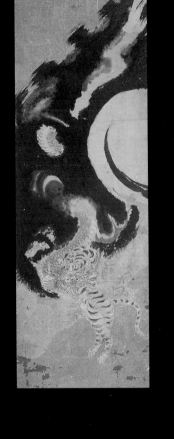

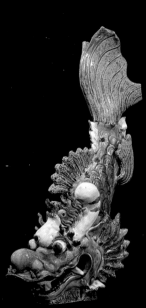

蔡仲平本

The flight of the phoenix: a silk panel (*opposite*) showing the bird among flowers and foliage, China, Sung Dynasty, 10th/12th century; a stylized bird on a lacquer bowl (*below*), China, Han Dynasty, 1st century B.C.

INNER REFLECTIONS ON AN OUTER WORLD

it is possible, within the limitations of Western thought and language, to describe the Tao and Taoism, though not very satisfactorily, and to identify its dominant symbols. Yet, there exists another vital, practical dimension: how can the Taoist best complete the equation between his inner self and the outer world? How can he best understand and harmonize the symbols set before him and within him to achieve the ideals of spiritual and sexual harmony?

A Ming Dynasty porcelain dish showing Taoist children at play, symbolizing the rebirth of adepts through the practice of Inner Alchemy, China, Ming Dynasty, 16th/17th century.

the ideal taoist

the ideals of Taoism are enshrined in the way of living of the Immortals, the hsien, *moving effortlessly in time and space, passing from earth to the heavens, utterly at one with the rhythms of the universe. As personifications of the finest aims of Taoism, such figures are the stuff of legend and myth, defined by the dominant symbols of the cosmos in perfect balance. Followers of Tao must be concerned with the cultivation of self and, although this may take place at the humblest level, learn to read the symbolism of the world around them as it is expressed in the polarization and, at the same time, the harmonies of* yin *and* yang.

A Taoist priest (*opposite*) announces to the gods of the universe that a ritual is about to begin and invites them to take part. In his hat he wears a 'flame', symbol of his inner energies now exteriorized in his communication with the heavens.

wu-wei

Harmony in the world (*opposite*): a soapstone seal (China, Ming Dynasty, 16th/17th century) depicts a scene from the 'Red Cliff' poem by Su Tung-p'o; the sense of peace evoked by the floating boat is repeated in this painting (*below*) of the *Hermit Fishing*, in which the sage has clearly chosen the way of tranquillity and non-action, China, 13th century.

the principle of wu-wei or 'non-action' is fundamental to Taoism. Attempts to interfere with the nature of things are bound to fail in the long term. But wu-wei is not complete inaction, it is more a way of practising sympathy with natural law, of putting oneself in tune with the basic rhythms of the universe. The principle is well illustrated by the story of the pine and the willow: after a heavy snow-fall the more rigid branches of the pine break under the weight of the snow, but the more supple willow branches bend, thus allowing the snow to fall to the ground.

The *Tao te ching* advocates, 'Do whatever consists of no action, then there will be order in the world.'

Quiet deliberation:
a silk painting of
the Eighteen
Scholars, China,
Sung Dynasty,
10th/13th century.

Sages at a poetry
contest (*opposite*) at
the Orchid Pavilion,
Ming Dynasty; wine
goblets drift on the
stream, supported
by leaves.

te

Lao-tzu divided the
Tao te ching *into two parts:*
the Tao, *or the way, and* Te, *'virtue'.*
But this does not mean 'virtue' in the Western
sense of moral and ethical correctness; it is rather the
innate virtue of the world — its essential properties.
The Taoist adept will strive for understanding of these
and this will inform his or her whole life and being.
True te *is the uncontrived, unforced naturalness*
with which the wise man will handle practical
affairs, putting his own wishes and
desires in line with the natural
flow of outside events
and phenomena.

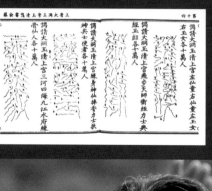

ch'i

the fusing of the individual life with the great cosmic spirit, Ch'i, is the object of the meditational, awakening exercises practised by the Taoist adept. This spirit informs the whole of nature, animate and inanimate alike, and is the subject of an elaborate system of symbols uniting the human body with its larger, cosmic context. The head corresponds to the heavens and the hair to the stars, the eyes to the sun and the ears to the moon. Blood, coursing through the veins, is a clear symbol for the rain, feeding the streams and rivers of the landscape, which is further symbolized by the bones (mountains) and orifices (valleys). By careful observation of nature, man's destiny may be properly understood.

謂請大洞玉清上宮左仙童右仙童左玉女右玉女各十萬人

An earnest practitioner (*opposite*) of *tai ch'i*, photographed in Shanghai, intent on aligning herself wih the vital *ch'i* forces, expressed in the inset diagram, China, Sung Dynasty, 10th/13th century.

the three crucibles

although the Taoist avoids set patterns
of behaviour and does not subscribe to a cut-
and-dried code of religious practice, certain
disciplines – the Inner Alchemy – are
recommended to aid the understanding of
self in relation to the great cosmic force.
Transformation of thought through
meditation eventually brings the adept into
alignment with the essential currents of
the universe. This awakening takes
place in three crucibles, the tan-t'ien.
The lowest is inside the belly, the middle one
behind the solar plexus and the third, where
the purified essence of the adept's
thought mingles with the cosmic
energies, in the head, symbol of
mountains and contact with the heavens.

The Taoist adept/yogi in meditation (*above*); his efforts to refine his spiritual energies are symbolized by the talisman (*opposite*), which is based on the gourd form of a crucible.

sexual harmonies

*t*he act of love provides Taoism with a
complex and extensive body of symbols, since
it so perfectly exemplifies the principles of
yin *and* yang. *Movement and position
during love-making are themselves described
in highly-charged symbolic language: 'wings
over the edge of the cliff'; 'cat and mouse
in the hole'; 'monkey hanging from pine
tree'; 'reversed flying ducks'.* Yin *and* yang
*imagery provides a natural code of description
for the form of the sexual organs. The male,*
yang, *may be 'red bird', 'dragon pillar',
or 'coral stem'. The female evokes softness
and openness: 'peach', 'peony', 'golden lotus',
the 'vase which receives'. For the Taoist, the
achievement of harmony in sexual relations
is a vital key to a long and fruitful life.*

Fusion of *ying*
and *yang (opposite)*:
*In the Garden on a
Rocky Seat*, ink
and colours
on silk, China,
Ch'ing Dynasty,
17th/18th century.

the full life...

the te is also 'living well', without stress and with the full enjoyment of one's mental and physical faculties. Patience and respect must be applied to the treatment of the body, but not necessarily through following the rules of conventional medicine or dietary control. The true Taoist will learn carefully from individual experience and from sympathetic observation of the world around; Taoist literature is full of allusions to the behaviour patterns of the natural world — mammals, insects, reptiles, plants, the properties of wind and water. The superior man does not have to be an ascetic: he will take pleasure in all experience.

The good life: two *blanc-de-chine* figures (*above*) of Mirth and Harmony, China, Ming Dynasty, 17th century; for the Taoist, aesthetic pleasure and harmony with nature are spiritually one (*opposite*), ink and colours on silk, China, Sung Dynasty, 13th century.

'The sage is for the belly and not for the eye.' – *Lao-tzu*

... and a healthy one

health *is a matter of great concern to the Taoist adept and, like sex, medicine provides a rich vocabulary of symbols. Indeed, perhaps the central symbol for the truly wise man, the Taoist sage, is the doctor, with his knowledge of the inner ebb and flow of the bodily forces and their relationship with those of the world outside. In more physical terms, the body is seen as a field of currents, based on the central circulation pattern, hence, the importance of acupuncture and the burning of the covering of dried moxa leaves on the skin in traditional Chinese medicine. Mental energies are likewise to be stimulated and cared for; the act of consulting the I-ching, for instance, is in itself beneficial.*

Care for man's inner force centres (*below*) ensures a continued thriving market in traditional herbal medicines, on sale here on a holy mountain at Emei, Sichuan, China (*opposite*).

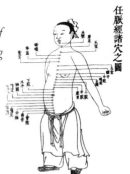

任脈經諸穴之圖

'In a home it is the site that matters.' – *Lao-tzu.*

the lie of the land

the vital streams of energy which enliven the body and the mind have their counterpart in the veins and streams of the natural world. Chinese landscape painting is characterized by the emphasis given to the 'dragon veins' which run in all directions; the artist will skilfully relate them to form an overall pattern to reveal the true lie of the land. Before a house is built many Chinese people will still call in the services of a geomancer, the feng-shui man, literally the 'wind and water' man, who will work out the direction and location of the structure in relation to the vital energy currents in the land. Such subtle relationships are also in the traditional Zen hard gardens, in which the rocks, representing mountains, seem to float in a 'sea' of immaculately raked gravel.

A geomancer, the *feng-shui* man, might express the forces of the land in such a diagram as this (*opposite right*) while the serious artist will seek to express the 'dragon veins', the flow of power through the landscape, in a harmonious composition (*opposite left*) – *Flowering Hills in the Height of Spring* by Lan Ying, China, Ming Dynasty, 17th century.

the tranquil taoist

according to the book of Chuang-tzu, an old man is seen by some followers of Confucius swimming in a raging torrent; suddenly, he disappears. The pupils of Confucius rush to save him, but the man reaches the bank entirely unaided. Asked how he had pulled off this remarkable feat of survival, the man replied that he had simply let himself go with the descending and ascending currents in the water. The true Taoist, in other words, moulds his senses, body and mind until they are at one with the currents of the world without.

Shen Chou (1427–1509) wrote a poem to accompany his ink and colour painting *Reading in the Autumn* which ends 'My spirit has gone wandering in the sky… Who can fathom it?' All is harmony among the *hsien* in the Taoist Heaven (*overleaf*), embroidered silk panel, China, 18th century.

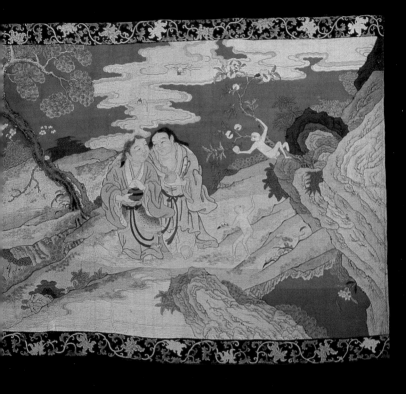

Sources of the illustrations

© 1996 Thames and Hudson Ltd, London

First published in the United States of America in 1996 by Thames and Hudson Inc., 500 Fifth Avenue, New York, New York 10110

Library of Congress Catalog Card Number 96-60180
ISBN 0-500-06024-X

Printed and bound in Slovenia